Searchlight
BOOKS

Do You Dig
Earth Science?

Figuring Out
Fossils

Sally M. Walker

Lerner Publications
Minneapolis

Lerner Publications Company
A division of Lerner Publishing Group, Inc.
241 First Avenue North
Minneapolis, MN 55401 USA

For reading levels and more information, look up this title at www.lernerbooks.com.

Library of Congress Cataloging-in-Publication Data

Walker, Sally M.
    Figuring out fossils / by Sally M. Walker.
        pages   cm — (Searchlight books™—Do you dig earth science?)
        Includes index.
        ISBN 978–1–4677–0019–1 (lib. bdg. : alk. paper)
        ISBN 978–1–4677–1020–6 (EB pdf)
        1. Fossils—Juvenile literature. 2. Paleontology—Juvenile literature. I. Title.
    QE714.5.W3449 2013
        560—dc23   2012013840

Manufactured in the United States of America
5-46490-12746-8/24/2018

Contents

Chapter 1

WHAT IS A FOSSIL?

Fossils are the hardened remains of plants and animals. Remains are parts left behind after plants or animals die. All fossils are old. Fossils are the traces and remains of plants and animals that lived more than ten thousand years ago.

These are the remains of an animal that lived long ago. What are remains?

There are many different kinds of fossils. Dinosaur bones are fossils. Dinosaur teeth are fossils too. Claws, eggs, and nests can be fossils. So can leaves, flower petals, and plant stems.

These fossil bones are from an animal called a saber-toothed tiger. Bones are only one kind of fossil.

Shells from ancient clams and snails are fossils. *Ancient* means "very old." The body parts of insects also can become fossils. Have you ever seen an insect that has turned into a fossil?

Clams are animals with hard shells. They live underwater.

Tracks and Trails

Ancient footprints are another kind of fossil. Scientists have found many ancient footprints. Some of the footprints are from human beings. Others are from dinosaurs.

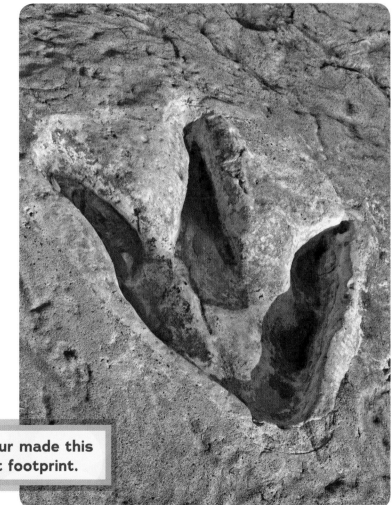

A dinosaur made this ancient footprint.

Animal trails can be fossils. Snails and worms make trails in mud. These trails show where an animal went.

This worm fossil shows the shape of a worm's body. It also shows trails the worm left on the ground.

Bones, tracks, and trails are all signs of life from long ago. And all of them can become fossils. But how do flower petals or dinosaur bones turn into fossils?

Leaf fossils are signs of plants that lived long ago.

Chapter 2

HOW DO FOSSILS FORM?

Fossils are plant and animal remains that have been naturally preserved. That means that they were saved without help from people. Most remains disappear over time. Other animals eat them or carry them away. Uneaten remains slowly rot. They become soft and fall apart.

These teeth became fossils. What happens to most plant and animal remains?

But sometimes, remains get buried. Then the remains are protected. They do not rot as quickly as remains that are not protected. They are hidden from animals that might eat them. The remains are also safe from water and wind. Water and wind can scatter remains. They can break remains apart.

Rock often surrounds dinosaur bones. Rock protects the bones.

Frozen Fossils

Ice can preserve remains. If ice covers the body of an animal that has died, the frozen body can last for many years. At one time, ice covered much of Earth. Many frozen plants and animals became fossils then.

Buried bones can last for a very long time. These buried dinosaur bones were discovered in China.

This is fossil hair from an animal called a woolly mammoth. Hair is a soft body part.

Ice preserves plants and animals very well. It can even preserve an animal's soft body parts, such as fur, skin, and muscles. Soft body parts don't usually become fossils. Most soft body parts rot quickly. So scientists are excited when they find fur, skin, or muscle fossils.

A Sticky Pit

Tar pits can preserve remains. Tar pits are pools full of asphalt. Asphalt is black and sticky. It comes from inside Earth. Sometimes animals fall into the asphalt. Then they get stuck. After a while, they die.

This pool of asphalt is at the La Brea Tar Pits. The La Brea Tar Pits are in Los Angeles, California. The animals are statues of creatures that lived long ago.

This saber-toothed tiger fossil was found at the La Brea Tar Pits.

When an animal dies in a tar pit, most of its body rots. But its teeth and bones do not rot. The asphalt preserves these hard body parts. When scientists dig in tar pits, they often find the teeth and bones of animals that lived long ago.

Buried under a Blanket of Bits

Sediments can preserve remains. Sediments are bits of mud, sand, stone, shell, or bone. Sediments cover plant and animal remains like a blanket. Most fossils are remains that were buried by sediments.

Millions of sediments piled up to make these layers.

This fossil was found at Fossil Butte National Monument. It is in Wyoming. Many people look for fossils in the layers there.

A blanket of sediments is called a layer. Some sediment layers are thin. Some sediment layers are thick. Layers can stack up on top of one another. Stacked sediment layers can be thousands of feet deep. Sediment layers can form on land or under water.

A deep stack of sediment layers is very heavy. The weight pushes the sediments together. Over time, chemicals in the sediments make them stick together. Then the sediments harden into rock. Rock that is made this way is called sedimentary rock. Fossils are often found in sedimentary rock.

Fossils are inside this sedimentary rock.

If remains are inside layers of sediments, they turn into rock along with the sediments. When plant or animal remains turn into rock, they become fossils.

This is a bird fossil. It is made out of rock.

Chapter 3

DO BONES REALLY TURN INTO STONE?

All bones have tiny holes in them. Sometimes groundwater soaks into the holes. Groundwater is water that is under the ground.

Groundwater often seeps into buried bones. What is groundwater?

Groundwater has dissolved chemicals in it. The chemicals join together inside the bones. When the chemicals join together, they form minerals. Minerals are the ingredients that make up rocks.

Rocks are made of minerals.

Hard Minerals

The minerals fill a bone's holes. The minerals become hard. They make the bone hard too. They also make the bone heavy. Sometimes the bone dissolves over time. But the minerals do not dissolve. They stay in the same place. They preserve the bone's shape. They become a fossil.

1. Fish bones are buried at the bottom of a lake.

2. Groundwater soaks into holes in the bones.

3. Chemicals in the groundwater form minerals inside the bones.

4. The minerals preserve the shape of the bones. The bones become a fossil.

This is one way fossils form.

A piece of wood has tiny spaces in it too. Water full of dissolved chemicals can soak into the spaces. The chemicals may become minerals. If the minerals form in the spaces, then the wood becomes a fossil.

Minerals turned these tree trunks into fossils.

Shell fossils are often molds. Molds are hollow spaces. Molds form after sediments bury plant or animal remains. Over time, the sediments turn into rock. Chemicals dissolve the remains. Then a hollow space is left behind. The mold shows the exact shape of the remains.

This is a fossil snail shell.

The fossil on the left is a mold. The fossil on the right is a cast.

Sometimes water and chemicals fill the hollow space. Minerals form inside the mold. When they do, they make another kind of fossil. A fossil that formed inside a mold is called a cast.

Chapter 4

FINDING FOSSILS

Fossils are found in many places. Some fossils are easy to find. People often find fossil shark teeth on beaches near the ocean.

People look for fossils on the beach. Some fossils are hard to find. Why are some fossils hard to find?

Other fossils are hard to find. Many fossils are hidden inside sedimentary rock. Scientists must dig through the rock to find them.

Sometimes fossils are hidden deep inside a rock. These fossils were hidden inside sedimentary rock.

Big and Small

A scientist who collects and studies fossils is called a paleontologist. Paleontologists study many kinds of fossils.

Fossils can be big or small. Some fossils are so small that paleontologists need microscopes to see them. Microscopes are tools that make small things look big.

The smallest fossils are very hard to see. Paleontologists use microscopes to study them.

Bigger fossils are often mixed with soil. Paleontologists sift the soil through a screen. This helps them uncover fossils. The soil passes through the holes, but the fossils do not.

Very large fossils such as shark teeth are easy to see. Paleontologists just pick them up.

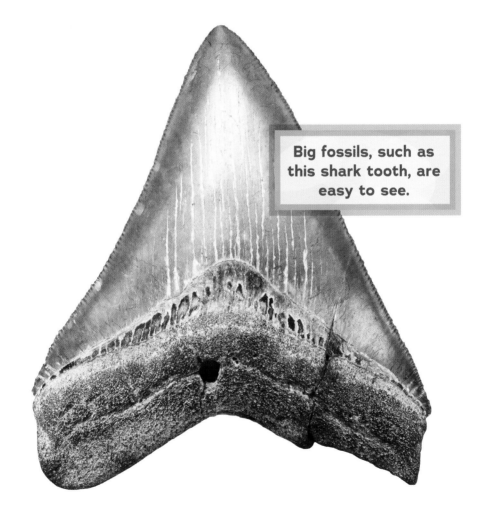

Big fossils, such as this shark tooth, are easy to see.

Moving Fragile Fossils

Sometimes a fossil is hidden inside a piece of rock. Then a paleontologist uses a special hammer to chip away the rock.

Some fossils are too heavy to lift. A large fossil may also be fragile. That means it breaks easily. Paleontologists must be careful not to break fragile fossils while moving them.

Fossils are often buried in rocks. This paleontologist is chipping at the rock to reach a fossil.

A paleontologist peels away the plaster shell that is protecting a fossil.

Paleontologists wrap fragile fossils to protect them. The paleontologists wet strips of cloth in a mixture of water and plaster. Plaster is a white material that gets hard as it dries. Paleontologists cover the fossil with the wet cloth strips. When the strips dry, they become a hard plaster shell. Paleontologists can safely move fossils inside plaster shells.

Chapter 5

WHY DO WE STUDY FOSSILS?

Paleontologists study fossils because they are important clues. Fossils can help paleontologists learn about ancient plants and animals.

Paleontologists study leaf fossils such as this one. What can paleontologists learn by studying fossils?

Fossil bones can tell paleontologists what an animal may have looked like. The paleontologists can figure out how big an animal was. They may be able to learn how the animal moved.

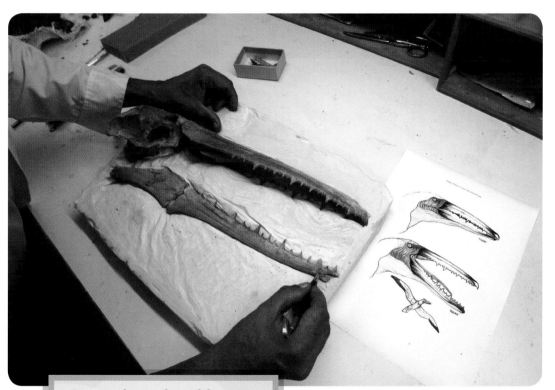

By studying fossil bones, paleontologists can learn about ancient animals. This paleontologist is working with a bird fossil.

The shapes of fossil teeth tell paleontologists what kinds of foods an animal may have eaten. Animals that eat meat have sharp teeth. Sharp teeth can slice meat the way knives do. Animals that eat plants have flat teeth. Flat teeth can chew and grind leaves.

Meat-eating dinosaurs had very sharp teeth.

Plants and Places

Fossils teach paleontologists about Earth's past. They give clues about what the weather and the land were like long ago. Some plants grow only in warm places. But sometimes fossils of those plants are found in a cold place. That tells us that at one time, the place was much warmer. Sometimes fish fossils are found in dry deserts. What do you think that means?

Sometimes fish fossils are found in dry areas. That tells us that water used to cover these areas.

Fossils Everywhere

Did you know that you use fossils almost every day? Sidewalks and some buildings are made of concrete. Concrete is made of crushed sedimentary rocks. Crushed sedimentary rocks are filled with fossils.

Have you ever written with chalk? Chalk is made of fossils too. The fossils that become chalk once lived in the sea. These fossils are very small. You would need a microscope to see them.

Many sidewalks are made of concrete.

Many science museums have fossils you can see.

Fossils tell part of Earth's story. Studying fossils is a fun way to learn about the past. Do you have a favorite fossil? What kind of story does it tell you?

Glossary

ancient: very old

asphalt: a sticky, black substance that comes from inside Earth. Asphalt is used to make roads.

cast: a fossil that forms inside a hollow space

fossil: a hardened part left behind after a plant or animal dies. Tracks, trails, and molds can also become fossils.

mineral: a solid substance that is not alive. Rocks are made of minerals.

mold: a hollow space that is left after buried remains have rotted away

paleontologist: a scientist who collects and studies fossils

preserved: saved from being destroyed

remains: parts left behind after plants or animals die

sedimentary rock: rock that forms when bits of mud, sand, stone, shell, or bone are squeezed together

sediments: bits of mud, sand, stone, shell, or bone

Learn More about Fossils

Books

Brecke, Nicole, and Patricia M. Stockland. *Dinosaurs and Other Prehistoric Creatures You Can Draw.* Minneapolis: Millbrook Press, 2010. If you like all things prehistoric, you'll love this fun lesson on how to draw dinos!

Greve, Tom. *Fossils, Uncovering the Past.* Vero Beach, FL: Rourke Publishing, 2011. Readers are introduced to fossils and their history in this informative book.

Parker, Steve. *100 Things You Should Know about Fossils.* Broomall, PA: Mason Crest, 2011. Tons of tidbits and fun facts fill this book on fossils.

Petersen, Christine. *Fantastic Fossils.* Edina, MN: Abdo Publishing, 2010. Bright images and clear explanations tell the story of fossils.

Walker, Sally M. *Mystery Fish: Secrets of the Coelacanth.* Minneapolis: Millbrook Press, 2006. Imagine what it would be like to find a living dinosaur! That's just what one woman did in the 1930s—and you can read all about it.

Websites

Enchanted Learning: Geology, Rocks, and Minerals
http://www.enchantedlearning.com/geology
This Enchanted Learning page is just the thing for budding Earth scientists.

Fossils for Kids
http://www.fossilsforkids.com
This site is a good jumping-off point for anyone wanting to know the basics of finding fossils.

Science News for Kids
http://www.sciencenewsforkids.org
This online magazine has articles all about science. It also has games, science fair news, and information on science experiments.

LERNER

SOURCE

Expand learning beyond the printed book. Download free, complementary educational resources for this book from our website, www.lerneresource.com.

Index

Photo Acknowledgments

The images in this book are used with the permission of: © The Natural History Museum, London, p. 4; © Martin Shields/Photo Researchers, Inc., p. 5; © Ken Lucas/Visuals Unlimited, Inc., pp. 6, 20; © Jill Stephenson/Alamy, p. 7; © DEA/G.Cigolini/De Agostini Picture Library/Getty Images, p. 8; © Harald Sund/Photographer's Choice/Getty Images, p. 9; © Ken Lucas/Visuals Unlimted/CORBIS, p. 10; © John Cancalosi/Peter Arnold/Getty Images, p. 11; © Xiong vijun/ImagineChina/ZUMA Press, p. 12; © Aristide Economopoulos/Star Ledger/CORBIS, p. 13; © Adambooth/Dreamstime.com, p. 14; © Albert Copley/Visuals Unlimited, Inc., pp. 15, 25; © Catonphoto/Dreamstime.com, p. 16; Photo by Arvid Aase of Bob and Bonnie Finney specimen/National Park Service, p. 17; © Albert J. Copley/Photodisc/Getty Images, p. 18; © Kevin Schafer/Peter Arnold/Getty Images, p. 19; © iStockphoto .com/Nikola Miljkovic, p. 21; © Laura Westlund/Independent Picture Service, p. 22; © PhotoLink/Photodisc/Getty Images, p. 23; © Carolina Biological/Visuals Unlimited/CORBIS, p. 24; © Glenn Nagel/Dreamstime.com, p. 26; © Gabbro/Alamy, p. 27; © Mauro Fermariello/Photo Researchers, Inc., p. 28; © Mark A. Schneider/Photo Researchers, Inc., p. 29; © Richard T. Nowitz/CORBIS, p. 30; © David McNew/Getty Images, p. 31; © John Cancalosi/Peter Arnold/Getty Images, p. 32; AP Photo/Martin Mejia, p. 33; © Raul Touzon/National Geographic/Getty Images, p. 34; © Jason Edwards/National Geographic/Getty Images, p. 35; © Ebby May/The Image Bank/Getty Images, p. 36; © Ingolf Pompe/LOOK/Getty Images, p. 37.

Front cover: © Jonathan Blair/CORBIS.

Main body text set in Adrianna Regular 14/20.
Typeface provided by Chank.